Rubáiyát

OF
OMAR KHAYYÁM

Rubáiyát
OF
OMAR KHAYYÁM

Translated by

EDWARD FITZGERALD

BARNES
&NOBLE
BOOKS
NEW YORK

This edition published by Barnes & Noble, Inc.

1993 Barnes & Noble Books

ISBN 1-56619-132-7

Designed by Charles Ziga, Ziga Design

Printed and bound in the United States of America

M 9 8 7 6 5 4 3 2 1

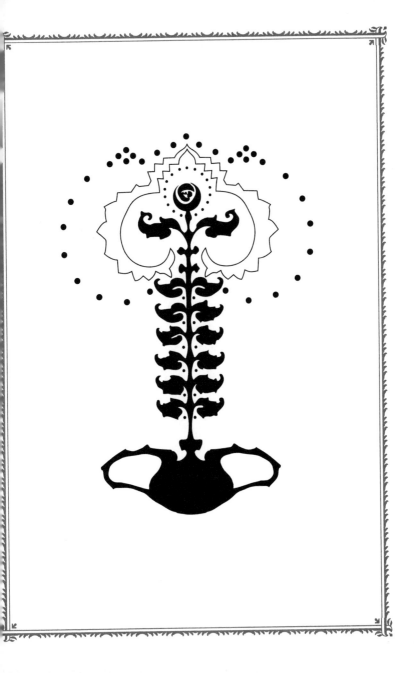

OMAR KHAYYÁM

The Astronomer-Poet of Persia

O mar Khayyám was born at Naishápúr in Khorassán in the latter half of our Eleventh, and died within the First Quarter of our Twelfth Century. The slender story of his life is curiously twined about that of two other very considerable Figures in their Time and Country: one of whom tells the Story of all Three. This was Nizám ul Mulk, Vizyr to Alp Arslan the Son, and Malik Shah the Grandson, of Toghrul Beg the Tartar, who has wrested Persia from the feeble Successor of Mahmúd the Great, and founded that Seljukian Dynasty which finally roused Europe into the Crusades. This Nizám ul Mulk, in his *Wasiyat*—or *Testament*—which he wrote and left as a Memorial for future Statesmen—relates the following, as quoted in the *Calcutta Review*, No. 59, from Mirkhond's History of the Assassins.

"One of the greatest of the wise men of Khorassán was the Imám Mowaffak of Naishápúr, a man highly honored and reverenced,—may God rejoice his soul: his illustrious years exceeded eighty-five, and it was the universal belief that every boy who read the Koran or studied the traditions in his presence, would assuredly attain to honor and happiness. For this cause did my father send me from Tús to Naishápúr with Abd-us-samad, the doctor of law, that I might employ myself in study and learning under the guidance of that illustrious teacher. Towards me he ever turned an eye of favor and kindness, and as his pupil I felt for him extreme affection and devotion, so that I passed four years in his service. When I first came there, I found two other pupils of mine own age newly arrived, Hakim Omar Khayyám, and the ill-fated Ben Sabbáh. Both were endowed with sharpness of wit and the highest natural powers and we three formed a close friendship together. When the Imám rose from his lectures, they used to join me, and we repeated to each other the lessons we had heard. Now Omar was a native of Naishápúr, while Hasan Ben Sabbáh's father was one

Ali, a man of austere life and practice, but heretical in his creed and doctrine. One day Hasan said to me and to Khayyám, 'It is a universal belief that the pupils of the Imám Mowaffak will attain to fortune. Now, even if we *all* do not attain thereto, without doubt one of us will; what then shall be our mutual pledge and bond?' We answered, 'Be it what you please.' 'Well,' he said, 'let us make a vow, that to whomsoever this fortune falls, he shall share it equally with the rest, and reserve no pre-eminence for himself.' 'Be it so,' we both replied, and on those terms we mutually pledged our words. Years rolled on, and I went from Khorassán to Transoxiana and wandered to Ghazni and Cabul; and when I returned, I was invested with office, and rose to be administrator of affairs during the Sultanate of Sultan Alp Arlsan.

"He goes on to state, that years passed by, and both his old school-friends found him out, and came and claimed a share in his good fortune, according to the school-day vow. The Vizier was generous and kept his word. Hasan demanded a place in the government, which the Sultan granted at the Vizier's request; but discontented with a gradual rise, he plunged into the maze of intrigue of an oriental court, and, failing in a base attempt to supplant his benefactor, he was disgraced and fell. After many mishaps and wanderings, Hasan became the head of the Persian sect of the *Ismailians*, —a party of fanatics who had long murmured in obscurity, but rose to an evil eminence under the guidance of his strong and evil will. In A. D. 1090, he seized the castle of Alamut, in the province of Rúdbar, which lies in the mountainous tract south of the Caspian Sea; and it was from this mountain home he obtained that evil celebrity among the Crusaders as the OLD MAN OF THE MOUNTAINS, and spread terror throughout the Mohammedan world; and it is yet disputed whether the word *Assassin,* which they have left in the language of modern Europe as their dark memorial, is derived from the *hashish,* or opiate of hemp-leaves (the Indian *bhang*), with which they maddened themselves to the sullen pitch of oriental desperation, or from the name of the founder of the dynasty, whom we have seen in his quiet collegiate days, at Naishápúr. One of the countless victims of the Assassin's dagger was Nizám-ul-Mulk himself, the old schoolboy friend.

"Omar Khayyám also came to the Vizier to claim his share; but not to ask for title or office. 'The greatest boon you can confer on me,' he said, 'is to let me live in a corner under the shadow of your future, to spread wide the advantages of Science, and pray for your long life and prosperity.' The Vizier tell us, that when he found Omar was really sincere in his refusal, he pressed him no further, but granted him a yearly pension of 1200 *mithkáls* of gold from the treasury of Naishápúr.

"At Naishápúr thus lived and died Omar Khayyám, 'busied,' adds the Vizier, 'in winning knowledge of every kind, and especially in Astronomy, wherein he attained to a very high pre-eminence. Under the Sultanate of Malik Shah, he came to Merv, and obtained great praise for his proficiency in science, and the Sultan showered favors upon him.'

"When the Malik Shah determined to reform the calendar, Omar was one of the eight learned men employed to do it; the result was the *Jaláli* era (so called from *Jalál-ud-din,* one of the King's names)—'a computation of time,' says Gibbon, 'which surpasses the Julian, and approaches the accuracy of the Gregorian style.' He is also the author of some astronomical tables, entitled Ziji-Maliksháhí, and the French have lately republished and translated an Arabic Treatise of his on Algebra.

"His Takhallus or poetical name (Khayyám) signifies a Tent-maker, and he is said to have at one time exercised that trade, perhaps before Nizám-ul-Mulk's generosity raised him to independence. Many Persian poets similarly derive their names from their occupations; thus we have Attár, 'a druggist,' Assár, 'an oil presser,' etc. Omar himself alludes to his name in the following whimsical lines:—

"'Khayyám, who stitched the tents of science,
Has fallen in grief's furnace and been suddenly burned;
The shears of Fate have cut the tent ropes of his life,
And the broker of Hope has sold him for nothing!'

"We have only one more anecdote to give of his Life, and that relates to the close; it is told in the anonymous preface which is sometimes prefixed to his poems,—

"It is written in the chronicles of the ancients that this King of the Wise, Omar Khayyám, died at Naishápúr in the year of the Hegira, 517 (A. D. 1123); in science he was unrivaled,—the very paragon of his age. Khwájah Nizámi of Samarcand, who was one of his pupils, relates the following story: 'I often used to hold conversations with my teacher, Omar Khayyám, in a garden; and one day he said to me, "My tomb shall be in a spot where the north wind may scatter roses over it." I wondered at the words he spake, but I knew that his were no idle words. Years after, when I chanced to revisit Naishápúr, I went to his final resting-place and lo! it was just outside a garden, and trees laden with fruit stretched their boughs over the garden wall, and dropped their flowers upon his tomb, so that the stone was hidden under them.'"

Though the Sultan "showered Favors upon him," Omar's Epicurean Audacity of Thought and Speech caused him to be regarded askance in his own Time and Country. He is said to have been especially hated and dreaded by the Sufis, whose Practise he ridiculed, and whose Faith amounts to little more than his own, when stript of the Mysticism and formal recognition of Islamism under which Omar would not hide. Their Poets, including Háfiz, who are (with the exception of Fırdausi) the most considerable in Persia, borrowed largely, indeed, of Omar's material, but turning it to a mystical Use more convenient to Themselves and the People they addressed; a People quite as quick of Doubt as of Belief; as keen of Bodily Sense as of Intellectual; and delighting in a cloudy composition of both, in which they could float luxuriously between Heaven and Earth, and this World and the next, on the wings of a poetical expression, that might serve indifferently for either. Omar was too honest of heart as well of Head for this. Having failed (however mistakenly) of finding any Providence but Destiny, and any World but This, he set about making the most of it; preferring rather to Soothe the Soul through

xiv

the Senses into Acquiescence with Things as he saw them, than to perplex it with vain disquietude after what they *might* be. It has been seen, however, that his Worldly Ambition was not exorbitant; and he very likely takes a humorous or perverse pleasure in exalting the gratification of Sense above that of the Intellect, in which he must have taken great delight, although it failed to answer the Questions in which he, in common with all men, was most vitally interested.

With regard to the present Translation, the original Rubáiyát (as, missing an Arabic Guttural, these *Tetrastichs* are more musically called) are independent Stanzas, consisting each of four Lines of equal though varied Prosody; sometimes *all* rhyming, but oftener (as here imitated) the third line a blank. Somewhat as in the Greek Alcaic, where the penultimate line seems to lift and suspend the Wave that falls over in the last. As usual with such kind of Oriental Verse, the Rubáiyát follow one another according to Alphabetic Rhyme—a strange succession of Grave and Gay. Those here selected are strung into something of an Eclogue, with perhaps a less than equal proportion of the "Drink and make-merry," which (genuine or not) recurs over-frequently in the Original. Either way, the Result is sad enough: saddest perhaps when most ostentatiously merry: more apt to move Sorrow than Anger toward the old Tent-maker, who, after vainly endeavoring to unshackle his Steps from Destiny, and to catch some authentic Glimpse of To-morrow, fell back upon To-day (which has outlasted so many To-morrows!) as the only ground he had got to stand upon, however momentarily slipping from under his feet.

There is some traditional presumption, and certainly the opinion of some learned men, in favor of Omar's being a Súfi—and even something of a Saint—those who please may so interpret his Wine and Cup-bearer. On the other hand, as there is far more historical certainty of his being a Philosopher, of scientific Insight and Ability far beyond that of the Age and Country he lived in; of such moderate worldly Ambition as becomes a Philosopher, and such moderate wants as rarely satisfy a Debauchee; other readers may be content to believe with me that, while the Wine Omar celebrates is simply the Juice of the Grape, he bragged more than he drank of it, in very defiance perhaps of that Spiritual Wine which left its Votaries sunk in Hypocrisy or Disgust.

— *Excerpted from the original Introduction by Edward FitzGerald*

Awake! for Morning in the
    Bowl of Night
Has flung the Stone that puts
    the Stars to Flight:
And lo! the Hunter of
    the East has caught
The Sultán's Turret in a
    Noose of Light.

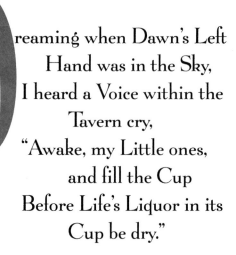

reaming when Dawn's Left
Hand was in the Sky,
I heard a Voice within the
Tavern cry,
"Awake, my Little ones,
and fill the Cup
Before Life's Liquor in its
Cup be dry."

And as the Cock crew, those
who stood before
The Tavern shouted—"Open
then the Door!
You know how little while
we have to stay,
And once departed, may
return no more."

Now the New Year reviving
        old Desires,
The thoughtful Soul to
        Solitude retires,
    Where the WHITE HAND
        OF MOSES on the Bough
Puts out, and Jesus from the
        Ground suspires.

Irám indeed is gone with all
its Rose,
And Jamshýd's Sevn'n-ring'd
Cup where no one
knows;
But still the Vine her
ancient Ruby yields,
And still a Garden by the
Water blows.

And David's Lips are lock't,
but in divine
High-piping Péhlevi, with
"Wine! Wine! Wine!
Red Wine!"— the Night-
ingale cries to the Rose
That yellow Cheek of hers
t'incarnadine.

Come, fill the Cup, and in the
Fire of Spring
The Winter Garment of
Repentence fling:
The Bird of Time has but
a little way
To fly—and Lo! the Bird is
on the Wing.

And look—a thousand Blossoms
with the Day
Woke—and a thousand scat-
ter'd into Clay:
And this first Summer
Month that brings the
Rose
Shall take Jamshýd and
Kaikobád away.

But come with old Khayyám
and leave the Lot
Of Kaikobád and Kaikhosrú
forgot:
Let Rustum lay about him
as he will,
Or Hátim Tai cry Supper—
heed them not.

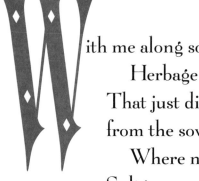ith me along some Strip of
    Herbage strown
That just divides the desert
from the sown,
    Where name of Slave and
Sultán scarce is known,
And pity Sultán Máhmúd on
his Throne.

Here with a Loaf of Bread
        beneath the Bough,
A Flask of Wine, a book of
        Verse—and Thou
Beside me singing in the
        Wilderness—
And Wilderness is Paradise
        enow.

XII

How sweet is mortal Sovranty!"—think some:
Others—"How blest the
Paradise to come!"
Ah, take the Cash in hand
and waive the Rest;
Oh, the brave Music of a
distant Drum!

ook to the Rose that blows
about us—"Lo,
Laughing," she says, "into
the World I blow:
At once the silken Tassel
of my Purse
Tear, and its Treasure on the
Garden throw."

The Worldly Hope men set
their Hearts upon
Turns Ashes—or it prospers;
and anon,
Like Snow upon the
Desert's dusty Face
Lighting a little Hour or
two—is gone.

And those who husbanded the
Golden Grain,
And those who flung it to
the Winds like Rain,
Alike to no such aureate
Earth are turn'd
As, buried once, Men want
dug up again.

Think, in this battered Cara-
vanserai
Whose Doorways are alter-
nate Night and Day,
How Sultán after Sultán
with his Pomp
Abode his Hour or two, and
went his way.

They say the Lion and the
　　　Lizard keep
The Courts where Jamshýd
　　　gloried and drank deep:
And Bahrám, that great
　　　Hunter—the Wild Ass
Stamps o'er his Head, and he
　　　lies fast asleep.

I sometimes think that never
blows so red
The Rose as where some
buried Caesar bled
That every Hyacinth the
Garden wears
Dropt in its Lap from some
once lovely Head.

nd this delightful Herb whose
tender Green
Fledges the River's Lip on
which we lean—
Ah, lean upon it lightly! for who knows
From what once Lovely Lip
it springs unseen!

Ah, my Belovéd, fill the cup
        that clears
TO-DAY of past Regrets and
        future Fears—
To-morrow?—Why, To-
        morrow I may be
Myself with Yesterday's
        Sev'n Thousand Years

Lo! some we loved, the love-
liest and the best
That Time and Fate of all
their Vintage prest,
Have drunk their Cup a
Round or two before,
And one by one crept silently
to Rest.

And we, that now make merry
in the Room
They left, and Summer dresses
in new Bloom,
Ourselves must we beneath
the Couch of Earth
Descend, ourselves to make
a Couch—for whom?

Ah, make the most of what we
    yet may spend,
Before we too into the Dust
    descend;
Dust into Dust, and under
    Dust, to lie,
Sans Wine, sans Song, sans
    Singer, and—sans End!

Alike for those who for TO-DAY
　　　prepare,
And those that after a TO-
　　MORROW stare,
　A Muezzín from the Tower
　　of Darkness cries,
"Fools! your Reward is
　　neither Here nor There!"

Why, all the Saints and Sages
who discuss'd
Of the Two Worlds so
learnedly, are thrust
Like foolish Prophets forth;
their Words to Scorn
Are scatter'd, and their
Mouths are stopt with
Dust.

Oh, come with old Khayyám,
    and leave the Wise
To talk; one thing is certain,
    that Life flies;
One thing is certain, and
    the Rest is Lies;
The Flower that once has
    blown for ever dies.

Myself when young did eagerly
frequent
Doctor and Saint, and heard
great Argument
About it and about, but
evermore
Came out by the same Door
as in I went.

With them the Seed of Wisdom
    did I sow,
And with my own hand
    labour'd it to grow:
And this was all the
    Harvest that I reap'd—
"I came like Water, and like
    Wind I go."

Into this Universe, and *why*
        not knowing,
Nor *whence,* like Water
        willy-nilly flowing!
And out of it, as Wind
        along the Waste,
I know not *whither,* willy-
        nilly blowing.

What, without asking, hither
hurried *whence?*
And, without asking, *whither*
hurried hence!
Another and another Cup
to drown
The memory of this Imperti-
nence!

U p from Earth's Centre through the Seventh Gate
I rose, and on the Throne of Saturn sate,
   And many Knots unravel'd by the Road;
But not the Knot of Human Death and Fate.

There was a Door to which I
found no Key;
There was a Veil past which
I could not see:
Some little Talk awhile of
ME and THEE
There seemed—and then no
more of THEE and ME.

hen to the rolling Heav'n
itself I cried,
Asking, "What Lamp had
Destiny to guide
Her little Children stumbling
in the Dark?"
And—"A blind understand-
ing!" Heaven replied.

Then to the earthen Bowl did I adjourn
My Lip the secret Well of Life to learn:
And Lip to Lip it murmur'd —"While you live
Drink!—for once dead you never shall return."

I think the Vessel, that with fugitive
    Articulation answer'd, once did live,
        And merry-make; and the cold Lip I kiss'd
    How many Kisses might it take—and give!

For in the Market-place, one
        Dusk of day,
I watch'd the Potter thumping
        his wet Clay:
And with its all obliterated
        Tongue
It murmur'd—"Gently,
        Brother, gently, pray!"

Ah, fill the Cup:—what boots
it to repeat
How time is slipping under-
neath our Feet:
Unborn TO-MORROW and
dead YESTERDAY
Why fret about them if
TO-DAY be sweet!

One Moment in Annihilation's
        Waste,
One Moment, of the Well
        of Life to taste—
The Stars are setting and
        the Caravan
Starts for the Dawn of
        Nothing—Oh, make
        haste!

How long, how long, in infinite
Pursuit
Of This and That endeavour
and dispute?
Better be merry with the
fruitful Grape
Than sadden after none, or
bitter, Fruit.

Y ou know, my Friends, how
        long since in my House
For a new Marriage I did
        make Carouse:
Divorced old barren
        Reason from my Bed,
And took the Daughter of
        the Vine to Spouse.

For "Is" and "IS-NOT" though
with Rule and Line,
And "UP-AND-DOWN" *with-
out,* I could define,
I yet in all I only cared to
know,
Was never deep in anything
but—Wine.

And lately, by the Tavern
Door agape,
Came stealing through the
Dusk an Angel Shape
Bearing a Vessel on his
Shoulder; and
He bid me taste of it; and
'twas—the Grape!

The Grape that can with Logic
absolute
The Two-and-Seventy jarring
Sects confute:
The subtle Alchemist that
in a Trice
Life's leaden Metal into Gold
transmute.

he mighty Mahmúd, the victorious Lord
That all the misbelieving and
black Horde
Of Fears and Sorrows
that infest the Soul
Scatters and slays with his
enchanted Sword.

But leave the Wise to wrangle,
and with me
The Quarrel of the Universe
let be:
And, in some corner of the
Hubbub coucht,
Make Game of that which
makes as much of Thee.

For in and out, above, about, below,
'Tis nothing but a Magic Shadow-show,
Play'd in a Box whose Candle is the Sun,
Round which we Phantom Figures come and go.

And if the Wine you drink, the
Lip you press,
End in the Nothing all Things
end in—Yes—
Then fancy while Thou
art, Thou art but what
Thou shalt be—Nothing—
Thou shalt not be less.

While the Rose blows along the
River Brink,
With old Khayyám the Ruby
Vintage drink:
And when the Angel with
his darker Draught
Draws up to Thee—take that,
and do not shrink.

'Tis all a Chequer-board of
Nights and Days
Where Destiny with Men
for Pieces plays:
Hither and thither moves,
and mates, and slays,
And one by one back in the
Closet lays.

he Ball no Question makes
of Ayes and Noes,
But Right or Left as strikes
the Player goes;
And He that toss'd Thee
down into the Field,
He knows about it all—He
knows—HE knows!

The Moving Finger writes:
    and, having writ,
Moves on: nor all thy Piety
    nor Wit
Shall lure it back to cancel
    half a Line,
Nor all thy Tears wash out
    a Word of it.

And that inverted Bowl we call
    The Sky,
Whereunder crawling coop't
    we live and die,
Lift not thy hands to *It* for
    help—for It
Rolls impotently on as Thou
    or I.

With Earth's first Clay They
     did the last Man's knead,
And then of the Last
     Harvest sow'd the Seed:
Yea, the first Morning of
     Creation wrote
What the Last Dawn of
     Reckoning shall read.

I tell Thee this—When, starting
from the Goal,
Over the shoulders of the
flaming Foal
Of Heav'n Parwin and
Mushtara they flung,
In my predestin'd Plot of
Dust and Soul

The Vine had struck a Fibre;
which about
If clings my Being—let the
Súfi flout;
Of my Base Metal may
be filed a Key,
That shall unlock the Door
he howls without.

And this I know: whether the
one True Light,
Kindle to Love, or Wrath
consume me quite,
One Glimpse of It within
the Tavern caught
Better than in the Temple
lost outright.

Oh Thou, who didst with
        Pitfall and with Gin
Beset the Road I was to
        wander in,
    Thou wilt not with Pre-
        destination round
Enmesh me, and impute my
        Fall to Sin?

Oh Thou, who Man of baser
Earth didst make
And who with Eden didst
devise the Snake;
For all the Sin wherewith
the Face of man
Is blacken'd, Man's Forgive-
ness give—and take!

Listen again. One Evening
at the Close
Of Ramazán, ere the better
Moon arose,
In that old Potter's Shop
I stood alone,
With the clay Population
round in Rows.

And, strange to tell, among that
　　　　Earthen Lot
　　Some could articulate, while
　　　　others not:
　　And suddenly one more
　　　　impatient cried—
　　"Who *is* the Potter, pray, and
　　　　who the Pot?"

Then said another—"Surely not
in vain
My substance from the common Earth was ta'en;
That He who subtly
wrought me into Shape
Should stamp me back to
common Earth again."

Another said—"Why, ne'er a
peevish Boy
Would break the Bowl from
which he drank in Joy;
Shall He that *made* the
Vessel in pure Love
And Fancy, in an after Rage
destroy!"

None answered this; but after
Silence spake
A Vessel of a more ungainly
Make:
"They sneer at me for
leaning all awry;
What! did the Hand then of
the Potter shake?"

Said one— "Folks of a surly
Tapster tell,
And daub his visage with the
Smoke of Hell;
They talk of some strict
Testing of us—Pish!
He's a Good Fellow and
'twill all be well."

Then said another with a long-
drawn Sigh,
"My Clay with long Oblivion
is gone dry:
But, fill me with the old
familiar Juice,
Methinks I might recover by-
and-bye!"

So while the Vessels one by
one were speaking,
One spied the little Crescent
all were seeking:
And then they jogged each
other, "Brother! Brother!
Hark to the Porter's Shoulder-
knot a-creaking!"

Ah, with the Grape my fading
Life provide,
And wash my Body whence
the Life has died,
And in a Winding-sheet
of Vine-leaf wrapt,
So bury me by some sweet
Garden side.

That ev'n my buried Ashes
such a Snare
Of Perfume shall fling up into
the Air,
As not a True Believer
passing by
But shall be overtaken un-
aware.

Indeed the Idols I have loved
    so long
Have done my Credit in
    Men's Eye much Wrong,
Have drowned my Honour
    in a shallow Cup,
And sold my Reputation for
    a Song.

Indeed, indeed, Repentance oft
        before
I swore—but was I sober
        when I swore?
And then and then came
        Spring, and Rose-in-hand
My thread-bare Penitence
        a-pieces tore.

And much as Wine has played
the Infidel,
And robb'd me of my Robe
of Honour—well,
I often wonder what the
Vintners buy
One half so precious as the
Goods they sell.

Alas, that Spring should vanish
    with the Rose!
That Youth's sweet-scented
    Manuscript should close!
The Nightingale that in the
    Branches sang,
Ah, whence, and whither flown
    again, who knows?

Ah, Love! could thou and I
    with Fate conspire
To grasp this sorry Scheme
    of Things entire,
Woud not we shatter it
    to bits and then
Re-mould it nearer to the
    Heart's Desire!

Ah, Moon of my Delight who
know'st no Wane,
The Moon of Heaven is
rising once again:
How oft hereafter rising
shall she look
Through this same Garden
after me—in vain!

And when Thyself with shining
     Foot shall pass
  Among the Guests Star-
     scattered on the Grass
  And in thy joyous Errand
     reach the Spot
Where I made one—turn
     down an empty Glass!
TAMÁM SHUD

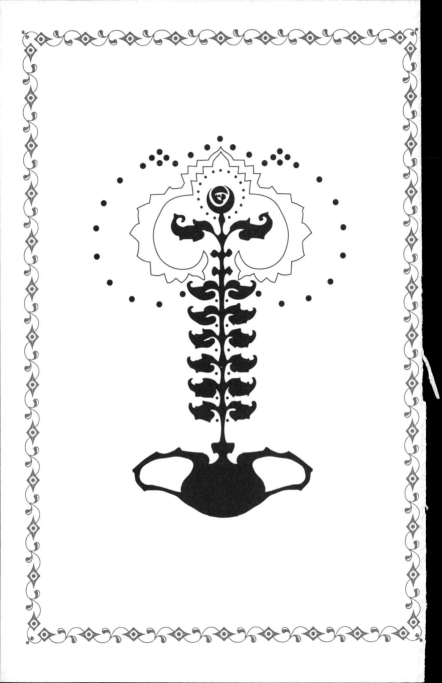